Kat*ie 2 Ifno's

Raintree is an imprint of Capstone Global Library Limited, a company incorporated in England and Wales having its registered office at 264 Banbury Road, Oxford, OX2 7DY – Registered company number: 6695582

www.raintree.co.uk
myorders@raintree.co.uk

Original illustrations © Capstone Global Library Limited 2021
Originated by Capstone Global Library Ltd
Printed and bound in India

978 1 4747 9454 1

British Library Cataloguing in Publication Data
A full catalogue record for this book is available from the British Library.

Contents

Katie's Neighbourhood

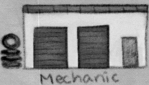

Police

Library

Mechanic

City Hall

Grocery Store

Post Office

Chapter 1

Fierce teeth

Katie Woo was at the zoo.

She told her mum, "I love

the alligator. He's so fierce!"

"Look at those teeth," said Katie's dad. "He must need a big toothbrush."

Katie laughed. "Yes, he must!"

"That reminds me," said Katie's mum. "You are seeing the dentist tomorrow. The hygienist will be cleaning your teeth."

"Cool," said Katie. "I love Ms Malek."

On the way to the dentist's, Katie saw Haley O'Hara and her five brothers and sisters. Katie told Haley, "I'm going to see Ms Malek."

Haley said, "Ms Malek told us we six kids have lost thirty-five baby teeth."

"Wow!" Katie smiled. "That's a lot of visits from the tooth fairy."

Chapter 2

At the dentist's

Katie and her mum

hurried to the dentist's.

The waiting room was a

fun place, filled with books

and toys.

Ms Malek greeted Katie with a big smile. Katie could see that Ms Malek was a great brusher and flosser.

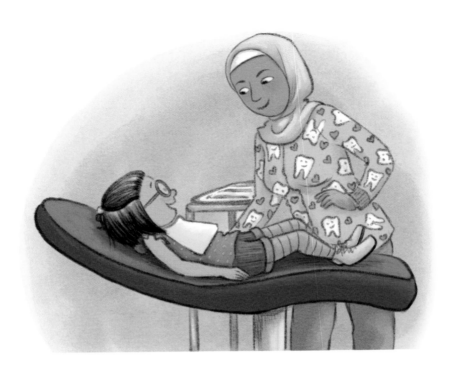

Katie liked having a ride

in the big blue chair.

"Now, open wide," said

Ms Malek.

Katie opened wide, like

an alligator.

Ms Malek used a tiny
mirror to look at each of
Katie's teeth.

"Looking good!" she said.
"I don't see any problems."

Ms Malek
cleaned Katie's
teeth with a cool
brush and paste.
Katie's smile
looked fabulous!

She asked Ms Malek,

"How do animals clean their

teeth?"

"Well, I know what a

hippo does," said Ms Malek.

"A hippo opens her mouth and a fish swims in. The fish eats the food between her teeth."

"Ew!" said Katie.

Katie's dentist, Mr Ali, looked at her teeth too. He told her, "Next time we will take some X-rays."

"Cool," said Katie. "I love how weird teeth look on X-rays!"

Katie had fun picking a new

toothbrush.

"I want pink," she decided.

"And cherry toothpaste."

Katie got a toy too.

Chapter 3
Big smile

On the way home, Katie

saw Pedro and JoJo. Katie told

them about hippos and fish.

"Ew!" said JoJo.

"Gross!" said Pedro.

Pedro told Katie, "The dentist at the zoo has to clean the tiger's teeth."

"Wow!" said Katie.

"He must be brave!"

"The tiger is not awake,"
said Pedro. "The dentist gives
him medicine to make him
sleep."

"Good idea!" said Katie.

Before bedtime, Katie

flossed and brushed her

teeth. She smiled at herself

in the mirror.

As Katie's dad tucked her into bed, she said, "When I grow up, maybe I will work at the zoo and clean the elephant's tusks."

"Wow!" said Katie's dad.

"You like to think big."

"I do!" agreed Katie.

She fell asleep with a

big smile.

Glossary

dentist someone who is trained in the care, treatment and repair of teeth and the fitting of false teeth

fabulous wonderful

fierce very strong or extreme

flosser a person who regularly uses dental floss, a thin strand of thread used to clean between the teeth

hygienist a person trained to know how to clean teeth

medicine a drug or other substance used in treating illness

paste a soft, creamy mixture

Katie's questions

1. What traits make a good dental hygienist? Would you like to be a dental hygienist? Why or why not?

2. Imagine you are in charge of cleaning an animal's teeth. Write a paragraph about it.

3. Taking care of your teeth is important. Make a poster that shows different ways to take care of your teeth. Draw a picture too!

4. Do you like to go to the dentist? Why or why not?

5. Teeth have different parts, including enamel, crown, dentin, pulp, root and gum. Research the parts of a tooth, then draw and label a diagram of a tooth.

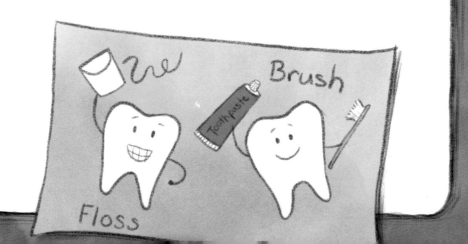

Katie interviews a dental hygienist

Katie: Hi Ms Malek! Thanks for telling me all about being a dental hygienist. What do you like best about your job?
Ms Malek: Because I work at a dentist's that is just for children, I get to meet and help a lot of great kids. I love teaching them how to take care of their teeth.

Katie: I know I love to come and see you! You are always fun to talk to.
Ms Malek: Well, thanks! I like talking to you too, Katie. But not everyone likes coming to see me. Some kids are nervous at the dentist. Then I take extra time to explain everything I'm doing and show them my tools.

Katie: What kind of tools?
Ms Malek: I have a little mirror that helps me see inside the mouth. I use a metal tool called a scaler to clean the teeth. Then I use a polisher to make the teeth as white and shiny as possible.

Katie: Where did you learn to use all those tools?

Ms Malek: At college! I have a two-year degree in dental hygiene. To be a hygienist, you also need to have a special licence to do the job. We must pass a test to earn that licence.

Katie: Do they teach you to wear fun uniforms at dental hygiene school?

Ms Malek: Ha! No, I discovered fun uniforms on my own. The shirt I wear is called a smock. I like ones with bright patterns. I also wear gloves, masks and glasses when I work. They *did* teach me about those things at college!

About the author

Fran Manushkin is the author of many popular picture books. There is a real Katie Woo – she's Fran's great-niece – but she never gets in half the trouble of the Katie Woo in the books. Fran writes in New York City, USA, without the help of her two naughty cats, Chaim and Goldy.

About the illustrator

Laura Zarrin spent her early childhood in the St. Louis, Missouri, area in the USA. There she explored creeks, woods and attic closets, climbed trees, and dug for artifacts in the garden, all in preparation for her future career as an archaeologist. She never became one, however, because she realised she's much happier drawing in the comfort of her own home while watching TV. When she was 12, her family moved to the Silicon Valley in California, where she still resides with her very logical husband and teen sons, and their illogical dog, Cody.